THE PARADOX OF INTELLIGENCE

Examining the Knowledge-Ignorance Dichotomy

ANTONIOS VALAMONTES

Dedication:

To those who dared to challenge me,
To the individuals who pushed me to think beyond the confines of
my comfort,
To the voices that questioned and provoked,
This work is dedicated to you.

You ignited a flame within me,
An insatiable curiosity to question everything I knew,
To unravel the layers of assumptions and biases,
and embrace the uncertainty that lies in the pursuit of truth.

Your unwavering commitment to intellectual growth,
Your relentless pursuit of knowledge, have inspired me to push
the boundaries of my understanding,
To confront my limitations and biases.

In the face of disagreement, you offered perspectives,
In the presence of doubt, you encouraged inquiry,
your unwavering belief in the power of critical thinking,
Has shaped the way I approach the world around me.

Through your challenges, I have learned resilience,
I have discovered the power of intellectual humility,
And I have realized that true growth lies in embracing discomfort,
and being willing to confront our own ignorance.

To you, the challengers, the questioners, and the skeptics,
I express my deepest gratitude,
For it is through your influence that I have grown,
and it is with humility and gratitude that I present this work.

May we continue to question, challenge, and seek,
For it is in the pursuit of knowledge and understanding,
That we strive towards a more enlightened world,
One where ignorance finds no fertile ground.

This work is dedicated to you, the catalysts of intellectual growth,
With heartfelt appreciation and admiration.

Antonios Valamontes

Abstract:

This thesis explores the paradoxical notion that the most educated and intelligent individuals can be simultaneously labeled as the most ignorant. While traditional beliefs associate education and intelligence with increased knowledge and awareness, this study delves into the complexities surrounding knowledge acquisition, personal biases, and the limitations of human understanding. By analyzing various psychological and sociological factors, we aim to shed light on the reasons behind this apparent contradiction and offer a nuanced perspective on the interplay between intelligence and ignorance.

References

By exploring the complex relationship between intelligence, education, and ignorance, this thesis aims to challenge conventional assumptions and foster a deeper understanding of human knowledge acquisition and the limitations therein. This research will encourage individuals to critically examine their biases and foster a more open-minded and informed society.

Chapter 1

Introduction

1.1 Background and Rationale

Education and intelligence are highly valued in today's knowledge-driven society, often synonymous with wisdom and awareness. The assumption that the most educated and intelligent individuals possess a greater understanding of the world seems intuitive at first glance. The paradox emerges – the most educated, smart people are sometimes found to be the most ignorant. This paradox challenges preconceived notions and raises intriguing questions about the nature of intelligence, knowledge acquisition, and potential human understanding limitations.

1.2 Research Objectives

The primary objective of this thesis is to explore and understand the paradoxical relationship between intelligence, education, and ignorance. By delving into the nuances of this paradox, we aim to uncover the underlying factors that contribute to the phenomenon, critically examining the limitations of knowledge acquisition, personal biases, and the potential role of societal and cultural influences. This research seeks to comprehensively understand the complex interplay between intelligence and ignorance and shed light on the underlying mechanisms contributing to this apparent contradiction.

1.3 Research Questions

The following research questions will be addressed throughout this thesis to guide our investigation:

1. What is the nature of intelligence, and how is it related to education?
2. How can we define ignorance in the context of educated individuals?
3. What psychological and sociological factors contribute to ignorance among the most educated?
4. What are the limits of knowledge acquisition, and how do they affect our understanding of the world?
5. What role do personal biases, such as confirmation bias and intellectual arrogance, play in perpetuating ignorance?
6. How do cultural and social influences shape the knowledge gaps among intelligent individuals?

1.4 Significance of the Study

This study holds both theoretical and practical significance. The theoretical implications lie in challenging the conventional wisdom that associates intelligence and education with superior knowledge and understanding. We aim to contribute to the growing body of literature on cognitive biases, knowledge acquisition, and the limitations of human cognition. The practical implications are relevant in today's polarized society, as it offers insights into the dynamics that hinder open-mindedness, critical thinking, and informed decision-making.

1.5 Scope and Limitations

It is important to note that this thesis does not claim to provide a definitive answer to the paradox of intelligence and ignorance. Rather, it seeks to offer a comprehensive exploration of the topic, drawing upon existing research, empirical evidence, and case studies. The scope of this study will primarily focus on psychological and sociological factors contributing to ignorance among the most educated individuals. While acknowledging the influence of cultural and societal factors, this thesis needs to provide an exhaustive analysis of all possible influences on knowledge acquisition and ignorance.

By setting the stage for the subsequent chapters, this introductory chapter outlines the purpose and significance of this research, establishes the research objectives and questions, and delineates the scope and limitations of the study. Through an in-depth examination of the paradox of intelligence and ignorance, this thesis aims to contribute to our understanding of human cognition, challenge existing assumptions, and stimulate further exploration in this intriguing field.

Chapter 2
The Nature of Intelligence and Education

2.1 Definitions and Dimensions of Intelligence

Intelligence is a multifaceted construct encompassing various cognitive abilities and capacities. Traditionally, it has been defined as the ability to reason, solve problems, learn from experience, and adapt to new situations. Psychometric approaches have sought to measure intelligence using standardized tests, such as IQ tests, which primarily assess analytical and logical reasoning abilities. However, it is important to recognize that intelligence extends beyond these cognitive aspects and encompasses other dimensions, such as creativity, emotional intelligence, and social intelligence. While there is no universally accepted definition, intelligence generally refers to the ability to learn, understand, reason, problem-solve, and adapt effectively to one's environment. It encompasses a range of cognitive abilities and skills contributing to an individual's capacity to function successfully in different domains.

2.1.1. Psychometric Approach:

One prominent approach to defining and measuring intelligence is psychometric, which focuses on assessing intellectual abilities through standardized tests. Psychometric tests, such as intelligence quotient (IQ) tests, measure general cognitive abilities and provide a numerical score representing an individual's intellectual functioning level. These tests assess verbal, mathematical, and spatial abilities, among others, and are designed to capture a broad spectrum of cognitive skills.

2.1.2. Multiple Intelligences Theory:

The theory of multiple intelligences proposed by Howard Gardner suggests that intelligence is not a singular entity but a collection of distinct and independent bits of intelligence. According to this theory, individuals possess different strengths and abilities across various domains. Gardner identified several bits of intelligence, including linguistic, logical-mathematical, spatial, musical, bodily-kinesthetic, interpersonal, intrapersonal, and naturalistic bits of intelligence. This theory broadens the traditional notion of intelligence beyond cognitive abilities, acknowledging other areas of human potential.

2.1.3. Triarchic Theory of Intelligence:

Developed by Robert Sternberg, the triarchic intelligence theory proposes that intelligence comprises three key components: analytical, creative, and practical intelligence. Analytical intelligence relates to problem-solving, critical thinking, and logical reasoning abilities. Creative intelligence involves the generation of novel ideas, original thinking, and the ability to adapt to new situations. Practical intelligence encompasses the skills necessary for successfully navigating real-world tasks, such as social competence, street smarts, and practical problem-solving abilities.

2.1.4. Emotional Intelligence:

Emotional intelligence (EI) refers to the ability to perceive, understand, manage, and use emotions effectively in oneself and others. Ay, Peter Salovey, and John Mayer proposed that EI encompasses self-awareness, empathy, emotional regulation, and interpersonal effectiveness. It is crucial in social interactions, decision-making, and personal well-being. EI emphasizes the importance of emotional awareness, competence, and cognitive abilities in determining intelligent behavior.

2.1.5. Contextual and Cultural Perspectives:

Cognitive abilities do not solely determine intelligence but are also influenced by cultural and contextual factors. Different cultures value and prioritize different types of intelligence, such as collectivist cultures emphasizing social skills and cooperation. Contextual factors, such as the demands of a specific environment or domain, can also shape the expression and assessment of intelligence. Recognizing the role of cultural and situational factors is essential for understanding intelligence within diverse populations.

It is important to note that these are just a few of the many theories and perspectives on intelligence. Intelligence research is rich and complex, with ongoing debates and discussions.

Different theories provide valuable insights into the diverse dimensions of intelligence and highlight the need for a comprehensive understanding that encompasses cognitive, emotional, cultural, and contextual aspects.

2.2 Role of Education in Knowledge Acquisition

Education is pivotal in acquiring knowledge and skills as it offers individuals structured learning opportunities encompassing various disciplines. Through formal education, individuals engage in a process that involves instruction, guidance, and assessment, developing critical thinking abilities, broadening intellectual perspectives, and cultivating a deeper comprehension of the world. By equipping individuals with the necessary tools to analyze information, evaluate evidence, and make informed judgments, education empowers them to navigate and interpret the vast realm of knowledge.

The role of education in knowledge acquisition is multifaceted and holds fundamental significance. Education is a well-organized system that facilitates acquiring, organizing, and practically applying knowledge and skills. Beyond the transfer of information, education plays a vital role in shaping individuals' intellectual, social, and emotional development. It provides a platform for personal growth, fostering the advancement of individuals in various domains of life. Education enables individuals to continuously expand their knowledge base and adapt to an ever-changing world by instilling a passion for learning and promoting critical inquiry. Furthermore, education cultivates the necessary competencies and capabilities to contribute to personal fulfillment and societal progress. Here are some key aspects of the role of education in knowledge acquisition:

2.2.1. Access to Information and Learning Resources:

Education provides access to a wide range of information and learning resources. Individuals gain exposure to various subjects, disciplines, and perspectives through formal education systems, such as schools, colleges, and universities. Educational institutions serve as repositories of knowledge, offering libraries, laboratories, and digital resources that enable students to explore and engage with information.

2.2.2. Development of Cognitive Skills and Critical Thinking:

Education fosters the development of cognitive skills, such as critical thinking, problem-solving, and analytical reasoning. It equips individuals with the tools and methods to critically assess information, evaluate arguments, and draw informed conclusions. Education encourages intellectual curiosity, the ability to ask questions, and the capacity to think independently, enabling individuals to acquire knowledge actively and engage in lifelong learning.

2.2.3. Acquisition of Domain-Specific Knowledge and Expertise:

Education provides individuals with specialized knowledge and expertise in specific domains. It offers structured learning experiences in mathematics, sciences, humanities, arts, and social sciences. Through formal instruction and guidance from qualified educators, individuals understand core concepts, theories, and methodologies within their chosen fields of study.

2.2.4. Skill Development and Practical Application:

Education goes beyond acquiring theoretical knowledge and emphasizes developing practical skills. Vocational and technical education and professional training programs equip individuals with practical skills for various careers and industries. These skills include technical proficiency, communication, teamwork, problem-solving, adaptability, and digital literacy. Education bridges the gap between theory and practice, preparing individuals to apply their knowledge in real-world contexts.

2.2.5. Social and Emotional Learning:

Education encompasses more than just academic knowledge; it also supports social and emotional learning. Educational environments provide opportunities for social interaction, collaboration, and the development of interpersonal skills. Education promotes empathy, respect, inclusivity, and cultural awareness, fostering social cohesion and understanding among individuals from diverse backgrounds. Additionally, education is crucial in nurturing emotional intelligence, self-awareness, and resilience.

2.2.6. Research and Innovation:

Education fuels research and innovation by fostering a culture of inquiry, exploration, and discovery. Educational institutions serve as hubs for scientific and scholarly research, contributing to expanding knowledge across various disciplines. Education encourages critical engagement with existing knowledge, encourages creativity and originality, and prepares individuals to contribute to advancements in their respective fields.

2.2.7. Empowerment and Societal Progress:

Education is a powerful tool for empowerment and societal progress. It equips individuals with the knowledge, skills, and capabilities necessary to participate in social, economic, and political spheres actively. Education can promote social mobility, reduce inequalities, and empower individuals to lead fulfilling and meaningful lives. Moreover, educated individuals contribute to the development and well-being of their communities, fostering economic growth, innovation, and social cohesion.

In summary, education plays a vital role in knowledge acquisition by providing access to information, fostering cognitive skills and critical thinking, facilitating the acquisition of domain-specific knowledge and skills, promoting social and emotional learning, supporting research and innovation, and empowering individuals and societies. By nurturing a lifelong love for learning and intellectual growth, education paves the way for personal development, societal progress, and the advancement of knowledge.

2.3 Cognitive Biases and Their Impact on Perception

Despite the potential benefits of education, highly educated individuals are susceptible to cognitive biases that can distort their perception of reality. Confirmation bias, for instance, leads individuals to seek and interpret information that confirms their preexisting beliefs while disregarding contradictory evidence. Similarly, availability heuristic and anchoring bias can influence decision-making by relying on readily available information or being influenced by initial reference points. These biases can hinder objectivity, leading to flawed reasoning and a limited understanding of complex issues.

Cognitive biases are systematic patterns of deviation from rationality or objective judgment in human thinking. These biases can significantly impact how we perceive and interpret information, leading to errors, distortions, and inaccuracies in our judgments and decision-making processes. Here, we will delve into some common cognitive biases and their impact on perception:

2.3.1. Confirmation Bias: This bias refers to seeking, interpreting, and favoring information that confirms our existing beliefs or hypotheses while disregarding or downplaying contradictory evidence. Confirmation bias can reinforce our preconceived notions and lead us to overlook alternative perspectives, distorting our perception of reality.

2.3.2. Availability Heuristic: The availability heuristic is a mental shortcut where we rely on immediate examples that come to mind when making judgments or decisions. It leads us to overestimate the importance or likelihood of events or information readily available in our memory. This bias can skew our perception by giving undue weight to vivid or easily accessible information while neglecting less salient but equally relevant data.

2.3.3. Anchoring Bias: Anchoring bias occurs when we rely too heavily on an initial piece of information, often called an anchor, when making judgments or estimates. The initial anchor can bias subsequent judgments, causing us to gravitate toward that initial reference point, even if it is arbitrary or irrelevant. This bias influences our perception by narrowing our range of possibilities and limiting our consideration of alternative viewpoints.

2.3.4. Halo Effect: The effect refers to the tendency to form a global impression of a person, object, or idea based on one positive characteristic or attribute. When the halo effect is present, our perception of someone or something is colored by a single positive trait, leading us to overlook or downplay other potentially relevant information. This bias can skew our perception by distorting our judgment based on a single characteristic.

2.3.5. Framing Effect: The framing effect occurs when our perception of a decision or situation is influenced by how it is presented or framed. How information is presented, including the context, wording, or emphasis, can influence our perception and subsequent decisions. This bias highlights that the same information, presented differently, can lead to different perceptions and outcomes.

2.3.6. Overconfidence Bias: Overconfidence bias is the tendency to overestimate our abilities, knowledge, or judgments. It leads us to have excessive confidence in our beliefs and judgments, often underestimating risks or overestimating our likelihood of success. This bias can impact our perception by distorting our confidence levels, leading us to ignore potential pitfalls or alternative viewpoints.

These are just a few examples of cognitive biases that influence our perception. Recognizing and being aware of these biases is essential as they can impact our decision-making, problem-solving, and overall understanding of the world. By acknowledging and actively challenging these biases, we can strive for more accurate and objective perception, leading to improved decision-making and a more comprehensive understanding of available information.

2.4 The Illusion of Expertise

Education and expertise are often synonymous, but the illusion of expertise arises when individuals overestimate their knowledge and competence in a domain. The Dunning-Kruger effect explains how those with low ability tend to overestimate their skills while true experts may underestimate their competence, leading to ignorance among the self-perceived knowledgeable.

Understanding intelligence, education's role in knowledge acquisition, and cognitive biases is crucial to unraveling the intelligence-ignorance paradox. This chapter lays the groundwork for exploring factors contributing to ignorance among the educated. Recognizing the complexities in intelligence and education fosters a nuanced understanding of knowledge, awareness, and ignorance.

The illusion of expertise occurs when individuals overestimate their knowledge in a domain, leading to overconfidence. This cognitive bias profoundly impacts decision-making, problem-solving, and learning. Here are some key details about the illusion of expertise:

2.4.1. Limited Self-Assessment: The illusion of expertise stems from the fact that individuals often have limited metacognitive abilities when assessing their knowledge and skills. They may lack the necessary self-awareness and accurate self-evaluation to recognize their limitations. As a result, they tend to believe they are more knowledgeable or skilled than they truly are.

2.4.2. Incomplete Knowledge: The illusion of expertise can arise when individuals possess a small amount of knowledge or information in a particular area but mistake it for comprehensive expertise. They may have some surface-level familiarity with a topic or have encountered a few key ideas, leading them to believe they deeply understand the subject. This illusion can hinder further learning and exploration, as individuals may become complacent with their limited knowledge.

2.4.3. Confirmation Bias: Confirmation bias, the tendency to seek out and interpret information confirming pre-existing beliefs or hypotheses, can contribute to the illusion of expertise. When individuals encounter information that aligns with their existing knowledge or opinions, they may perceive it as further confirmation of their expertise. At the same time, they may disregard or downplay contradictory information that challenges their beliefs, reinforcing the illusion.

2.4.4. Overestimation of Competence: The illusion of expertise often leads individuals to overestimate their competence and underestimate the complexity of a task or domain. They may take on challenges or make decisions based on their inflated perception of expertise, resulting in poor outcomes, errors, or inefficient problem-solving. This overconfidence can hinder personal growth and learning, as individuals may be less inclined to seek further knowledge or expertise in areas where they believe they are already proficient.

2.4.5. Implications for Decision-Making: The illusion of expertise can significantly affect decision-making processes. When individuals overestimate their expertise, they may be less likely to seek out diverse perspectives or consult with others with expertise in the domain, limiting their ability to make well-informed decisions and leading to suboptimal outcomes.

2.4.6. Mitigating the Illusion: Recognizing and mitigating the illusion of expertise requires fostering a mindset of humility, intellectual curiosity, and a willingness to engage in continuous learning. Encouraging individuals to self-reflect, seek constructive feedback, and critically evaluate their knowledge and skills can help counteract the bias. Additionally, creating environments that value and reward intellectual growth and collaboration can promote a more accurate assessment of expertise.

Understanding the illusion of expertise is essential for individuals and organizations to make better-informed decisions and foster a culture of continuous learning. By being aware of our cognitive biases and the limitations of our knowledge, we can strive for a more accurate assessment of our expertise and actively pursue further learning and development.

Chapter 3
The Paradox of Ignorance

3.1 The Dunning-Kruger Effect

The Dunning-Kruger effect, a well-documented cognitive bias, provides valuable insights into the paradox of ignorance among the most educated individuals. This effect describes the tendency of individuals with low competence in a specific domain to overestimate their abilities, while those with higher competence may underestimate their abilities. This phenomenon highlights the disconnect between perceived knowledge and actual expertise, illustrating how ignorance can prevail even among intelligent individuals who lack self-awareness regarding their limitations.

The effect was first described in a seminal study by psychologists David Dunning and Justin Kruger in 1999. They found that participants who scored low on a test of humor, grammar, or logic consistently overestimated their performance, rating themselves above average. Conversely, participants who scored high on the same tests tended to underestimate their performance, rating themselves below average. The researchers attributed this bias to a need for metacognitive skills, meaning that individuals less competent in a domain may not accurately assess their abilities.

Several factors contribute to the Dunning-Kruger effect. One factor is a lack of knowledge or experience in a particular domain, which can lead to a false sense of confidence. When individuals have a limited understanding of a subject, they may need to possess the necessary skills to evaluate their performance accurately, which can result in overestimating their abilities due to a lack of awareness of what they need to know.

Another factor is cognitive biases, such as confirmation bias, where individuals seek information that confirms their beliefs or abilities while ignoring contradictory evidence. This bias can reinforce the inaccurate self-perceptions of individuals with low competence as they selectively attend to information that supports their overestimation of their abilities.

The Dunning-Kruger effect has important implications across various areas of life. In academic settings, it can affect students' self-assessment of their knowledge and skills, potentially leading to poor academic performance or a reluctance to seek help or feedback. In the workplace, individuals affected by the Dunning-Kruger effect may exhibit overconfidence and resist constructive criticism, hindering their professional growth and collaboration.

Mitigating the Dunning-Kruger effect requires developing metacognitive skills, which involve self-reflection, self-awareness, and assessing one's abilities accurately. Encouraging individuals to seek objective feedback, engage in self-assessment exercises, and provide continuous learning and skill development opportunities can help combat the cognitive biases contributing to the Dunning-Kruger effect.

Overall, the Dunning-Kruger effect highlights the inherent challenges in accurately assessing competence. Recognizing this phenomenon can enhance our understanding of human cognition and decision-making and promote a more humble and reflective approach to learning and expertise.

3.2 Overconfidence and Confirmation Bias

Overconfidence and confirmation bias are two cognitive biases that significantly influence thinking and decision-making, contributing to ignorance. Due to their extensive knowledge and intellectual accomplishments, highly educated individuals may exhibit overconfidence in their beliefs and ideas. This overconfidence can lead to a dismissive attitude towards alternative viewpoints and a reluctance to evaluate new information critically. Moreover, confirmation bias exacerbates the problem as it reinforces existing beliefs by selectively seeking and interpreting information that aligns with them, limiting exposure to diverse perspectives.

These biases, overconfidence, and confirmation bias profoundly impact our cognitive processes and decision-making. They play a significant role in perpetuating ignorance and hindering knowledge acquisition.

Let us delve into each bias and its impact in more detail:

3.2.1. Overconfidence Bias:

Overconfidence bias refers to the tendency for individuals to have more confidence in their judgments, abilities, or beliefs than is objectively justified. It involves an inflated perception of knowledge, skills, or predictive abilities. People affected by overconfidence bias often underestimate the risks or challenges of a particular situation and overestimate their likelihood of success.

This bias can have several consequences. It can lead individuals to take on tasks or make decisions without adequately considering potential pitfalls or alternative viewpoints. Overconfidence bias can also hinder learning and personal growth, as individuals may become complacent with their current knowledge or skills, believing that further improvement is unnecessary. Additionally, overconfidence bias can contribute to poor decision-making and suboptimal outcomes, as individuals may need to seek out diverse perspectives or consider contradictory evidence.

3.2.2. Confirmation Bias:

Confirmation bias refers to seeking, interpreting, and remembering information that confirms one's pre-existing beliefs or hypotheses while disregarding or downplaying contradictory evidence. Individuals affected by confirmation bias actively seek out information that aligns with their existing views and filter or ignores information that challenges them.

Confirmation bias can have a significant impact on our perception and decision-making. By selectively attending to information that supports our preconceived notions, we may miss out on alternative perspectives, evidence, or viewpoints that provide a more accurate or comprehensive understanding of a situation. This bias can reinforce existing beliefs, even based on limited or flawed information. As a result, confirmation bias can lead to closed-mindedness, a lack of critical thinking, and the perpetuation of misconceptions or stereotypes.

Both overconfidence bias and confirmation bias can work in tandem, amplifying each other's effects. Overconfidence bias can lead individuals to seek out and interpret information that confirms their overinflated beliefs, further reinforcing confirmation bias. This combination can result in a strong attachment to preconceived ideas, limited consideration of alternative viewpoints, and resistance to change.

Recognizing and mitigating the impact of overconfidence and confirmation biases is essential for making rational and well-informed decisions. It requires cultivating self-awareness, actively seeking out diverse perspectives and evidence, and being open to revising our beliefs in light of new information. By challenging our assumptions and actively considering opposing viewpoints, we can reduce the influence of these biases and make more objective judgments.

3.3 Intellectual Arrogance and Closed-Mindedness

Often observed in highly educated individuals, intellectual arrogance can contribute to ignorance. Accumulating knowledge and academic achievements may lead to a sense of superiority, fostering a closed-minded attitude. Believing their understanding of a subject to be comprehensive, they may dismiss alternative viewpoints and resist ideas that challenge their existing knowledge. As a result, their ignorance persists, impeding intellectual growth and limiting their understanding.

Intellectual arrogance and closed-mindedness are attitudes and behaviors that hinder intellectual growth, limit understanding, and contribute to ignorance. These biases prevent individuals from embracing new information and perspectives, maintaining a rigid stance that inhibits their ability to expand knowledge and engage in meaningful dialogue. Overcoming these attitudes is crucial to fostering a more open and receptive mindset, encouraging intellectual growth and a deeper understanding of the world's complexities. Let us explore each concept in more detail:

3.3.1. Intellectual Arrogance:

Intellectual arrogance refers to excessive superiority or unwarranted confidence in one's intellectual abilities, knowledge, or ideas. Individuals with intellectual arrogance tend to believe that their perspectives, beliefs, or knowledge are inherently superior to others. They may dismiss or belittle alternative viewpoints, considering them inferior or irrelevant. Intellectual arrogance can lead to a closed-minded approach where individuals become less receptive to new ideas, information, or perspectives. This attitude can create a barrier to learning and intellectual growth since it discourages critical thinking, genuine dialogue, and the exploration of diverse viewpoints. Intellectual arrogance often results in a stagnant intellectual environment, where individuals are less open to questioning their assumptions or considering alternative interpretations.

3.3.2. Closed-Mindedness:

Closed-mindedness is the unwillingness or inability to consider or entertain ideas, perspectives, or evidence contradicting one's pre-existing beliefs or worldview. Closed-minded individuals tend to have rigid thinking patterns and resist challenging their established ideas. They may selectively filter out or dismiss information that challenges their beliefs, reinforcing their existing biases and limiting intellectual exploration.

Closed-mindedness can hinder intellectual development by impeding the acquisition of new knowledge and alternative viewpoints. It stifles curiosity and inhibits critical thinking, preventing individuals from engaging in meaningful discourse or expanding their understanding. Closed-mindedness can create echo chambers or intellectual bubbles, where individuals only surround themselves with like-minded people or information that reinforces their biases, leading to a narrow and limited perspective.

The combination of intellectual arrogance and closed-mindedness can intensify the barriers to knowledge acquisition and perpetuate ignorance. When individuals are overly confident in their intellectual abilities and simultaneously closed off to different ideas and perspectives, they become resistant to growth and less receptive to challenging their beliefs or expanding their understanding.

Overcoming intellectual arrogance and closed-mindedness requires self-reflection, humility, and a genuine openness to consider alternative viewpoints. It involves actively seeking diverse perspectives, engaging in constructive dialogue, and cultivating a willingness to challenge and question one's assumptions. By fostering intellectual humility and embracing a more open-minded approach, individuals can break free from the limitations of arrogance and closed-mindedness, allowing for greater intellectual growth and a deeper understanding of the world around them.

3.4 Cultural and Social Influences on Ignorance

Ignorance among highly educated individuals is not solely rooted in individual biases; broader cultural and social factors also significantly influence it. Cultural norms, social group dynamics, and ideological affiliations can shape an individual's understanding and perception of knowledge. These factors contribute to ignorance by fostering conformity to societal expectations, promoting intellectual groupthink, and reinforcing specific narratives within particular social circles. As a result, critical thinking, open-mindedness, and the willingness to engage with alternative viewpoints may be discouraged.

This chapter explores various factors contributing to ignorance among the most educated individuals, including the Dunning-Kruger effect, overconfidence, confirmation bias, intellectual arrogance, and cultural and social influences. By examining these psychological and sociological influences, we gain insights into the complex interplay that leads to ignorance despite high levels of intelligence and education. Understanding these factors is crucial for unraveling the persistence of ignorance and developing strategies and interventions to promote a more open, informed, and intellectually humble society.

Cultural and social influences significantly shape individuals' perspectives, beliefs, and knowledge, contributing to and perpetuating ignorance. Recognizing the impact of these influences is essential for addressing the root causes of ignorance and fostering a more enlightened society. By examining the role of culture, social dynamics, and ideological affiliations, we can better understand the multifaceted nature of ignorance and work towards creating an environment that promotes critical thinking, open-mindedness, and the pursuit of knowledge. Let us explore the impact of cultural and social influences on ignorance:

3.4.1. Cultural Influences:

Cultural factors, such as traditions, customs, and societal norms, can influence the knowledge and beliefs within a particular group or community. However, these cultural influences can sometimes reinforce ignorance by limiting exposure to diverse perspectives, ideas, or information. Cultural practices or beliefs that discourage critical thinking, skepticism, or questioning the established norms can hinder intellectual growth and perpetuate ignorance.

Moreover, cultural biases and stereotypes can lead to the perpetuation of misinformation or prejudice. When individuals conform to cultural biases without critically examining them, it can result in accepting false or misleading information, leading to ignorance about certain topics or groups of people. Cultural factors can shape individuals' understanding of the world, but if these influences discourage open-mindedness, curiosity, and the pursuit of knowledge, they can contribute to ignorance.

3.4.2. Social Influences:

Social influences, including peer pressure, groupthink, and social conformity, can impact individuals' willingness to explore new ideas or challenge prevailing beliefs. People often seek social validation and acceptance, leading to adopting beliefs or viewpoints without proper critical evaluation. In such cases, social influences can reinforce ignorance by discouraging independent thinking and preventing individuals from considering alternative perspectives.

Social media and online communities also play a significant role in shaping knowledge and fostering ignorance. These platforms can create echo chambers, where individuals are exposed only to information and viewpoints that align with their existing beliefs, resulting in a limited understanding of complex issues and a lack of exposure to diverse perspectives. Additionally, the rapid spread of misinformation on social media can perpetuate ignorance, as false or misleading information can easily go unchecked and become widely accepted.

It is important to note that cultural and social influences are not inherently negative or detrimental to knowledge acquisition. They can also foster learning, open-mindedness, and the exchange of ideas. By promoting cultural diversity, encouraging critical thinking, creating spaces for respectful dialogue, and sharing diverse perspectives, cultural and social influences can be harnessed to combat ignorance rather than perpetuate it.

To address ignorance influenced by cultural and social factors, individuals must actively seek out diverse viewpoints, question prevailing beliefs, and critically evaluate the information they encounter. Embracing cultural diversity, fostering open dialogue, and promoting critical thinking within societies can contribute to a more informed and knowledgeable collective. By recognizing the influence of cultural and social factors on ignorance, we can work towards creating inclusive and intellectually stimulating environments that encourage continuous learning and the pursuit of knowledge.

Chapter 4

The Limits of Knowledge

4.1 Theoretical Foundations: The Epistemological Challenge

Knowledge acquisition has limitations. Epistemology raises questions about the nature and extent of human understanding. It explores foundationalism, coherentism, and skepticism, highlighting challenges in attaining absolute knowledge. These perspectives remind us that our cognitive abilities and perspectives shape our understanding of the world.

Theoretical foundations are crucial for guiding research. The epistemological challenge is key in examining the paradox of ignorance among the highly educated. Epistemology explores knowledge's nature, origins, and limits, questioning how it is acquired, justified, and shared.

The epistemological challenge revolves around understanding the complexities of knowledge and the factors contributing to ignorance despite high levels of education and intelligence. This challenge requires critically examining how knowledge is constructed, validated, and transmitted within various domains and social contexts. It invites us to question the underlying assumptions and biases that may hinder the acquisition and application of knowledge, particularly among individuals who are considered highly educated.

One key aspect of the epistemological challenge is recognizing that knowledge is not static and universally objective. Instead, it is influenced by subjective interpretations, cultural perspectives, and social dynamics. Different disciplines and fields of study often employ distinct epistemological frameworks that shape how knowledge is defined, evaluated, and disseminated. Acknowledging these diverse epistemological perspectives is essential for understanding the complex nature of knowledge and the potential for ignorance within specific intellectual domains.

Furthermore, the epistemological challenge prompts us to explore the role of power structures and social hierarchies in knowledge production and dissemination. It raises questions about who can define what counts as knowledge, whose voices are marginalized or excluded, and how these dynamics contribute to the persistence of ignorance. By critically examining the social, political, and economic contexts in which knowledge is produced, we gain insights into the systemic factors that may perpetuate ignorance among the most educated individuals.

Addressing the epistemological challenge requires a multidisciplinary approach integrating philosophical inquiry, social theory, and empirical research. Researchers can develop a nuanced understanding of how knowledge is constructed, challenged, and disseminated by engaging with various theoretical perspectives. This understanding forms the basis for uncovering the underlying causes of ignorance among highly educated individuals and proposing strategies to promote a more enlightened and intellectually humble society.

In summary, the epistemological challenge forms the theoretical foundation for exploring the paradox of ignorance among the most educated individuals. It compels researchers to critically examine the nature of knowledge, the influence of cultural and social factors, and the power dynamics that shape knowledge production and dissemination. By addressing this challenge, we can gain deeper insights into the complex interplay between knowledge and ignorance and work towards fostering a more informed and intellectually humble society.

4.2 Uncertainty and Incomplete Information

Uncertainty and incomplete information are inherent aspects of the human condition that significantly impact the pursuit of knowledge. In various domains, achieving complete certainty is often unattainable, and gaps in knowledge emerge due to the vastness and complexity of the world. Even highly educated individuals encounter situations where information is scarce, ambiguous, or evolving. Uncertainty and incomplete information contribute to ignorance, as individuals must navigate uncertainties and make decisions based on incomplete knowledge. These factors underscore the limitations of our understanding and the challenges we face in acquiring comprehensive and accurate knowledge.

Uncertainty refers to the lack of certainty or predictability in a given situation or the limitations of our knowledge about a particular topic. It arises from various sources, such as limited data, complex systems, and unpredictable events. Uncertainty can hinder our ability to make informed judgments and draw definitive conclusions. It often necessitates a recognition of the boundaries of our knowledge and accepting the potential for error or ambiguity.

Incomplete information, on the other hand, refers to the lack of comprehensive or exhaustive data or knowledge about a particular subject. It occurs when relevant information is missing, inaccessible, or difficult to obtain. Incomplete information can lead to gaps in our understanding, making it challenging to form a complete and accurate picture of a given situation or phenomenon. It highlights the need for ongoing research, data collection, and critical analysis to reduce informational gaps and improve decision-making processes.

Both uncertainty and incomplete information pose significant challenges to knowledge acquisition and decision-making. They require individuals to navigate a landscape of unknowns, probabilities, and potential biases. In the face of uncertainty and incomplete information, individuals must rely on various strategies, such as critical thinking, reasoning, and gathering additional evidence, to mitigate the impact of these limitations on their understanding.

Furthermore, recognizing the presence of uncertainty and incomplete information is essential for maintaining intellectual humility. It reminds us that knowledge is a dynamic and evolving process, subject to revision and refinement as new information becomes available. Embracing uncertainty and acknowledging the limits of our knowledge can foster a more open-minded and receptive attitude, allowing for the exploration of alternative perspectives and the incorporation of new evidence.

In summary, uncertainty and incomplete information are inherent challenges in acquiring knowledge. They highlight the limitations of our understanding and the need for intellectual humility. Recognizing and addressing these challenges can enhance our ability to navigate uncertainty, mitigate biases, and continually refine our understanding of the world.

4.3 The Boundaries of Disciplinary Knowledge

Disciplinary knowledge, often specialized and focused on specific fields, is valuable and limiting. While specialization allows for in-depth exploration within a specific domain, it also establishes boundaries that restrict understanding beyond one's area of expertise. Highly educated individuals may possess extensive knowledge within their specialized field, but their understanding of other subjects may be lacking. This limitation contributes to their ignorance in areas outside their expertise, perpetuating the paradox of knowledge and ignorance among intelligent individuals.

Disciplinary knowledge encompasses expertise within academic fields or disciplines, crucial in advancing understanding within specific domains. However, it is important to acknowledge the boundaries and limitations of disciplinary knowledge.

The scope and focus of each field of study shape the boundaries of disciplinary knowledge. Disciplines have theories, methods, and concepts that guide inquiry and contribute to understanding phenomena within their domain. These boundaries provide structure for organizing knowledge, conducting research, and fostering intellectual growth. Nevertheless, they also create limitations by defining what falls within and outside the scope of a discipline.

The boundaries of disciplinary knowledge can lead to specialization and fragmentation as different disciplines develop their unique approaches, language, and methodologies. This specialization enables in-depth exploration and expertise within a specific area but can hinder interdisciplinary collaboration and a holistic understanding. It is crucial to recognize that disciplinary knowledge, while valuable, represents only a partial view of reality, as it focuses on specific aspects or dimensions of a subject.

Moreover, disciplinary knowledge is influenced by historical, cultural, and social factors, which shape the paradigms, theories, and methodologies employed within a discipline. Different disciplines may have varying perspectives, assumptions, and biases that shape their understanding of phenomena. The boundaries of disciplinary knowledge can limit exposure to alternative viewpoints, interdisciplinary connections, and novel approaches that may exist outside the confines of a specific discipline.

Recognizing the boundaries of disciplinary knowledge is essential for cultivating a more comprehensive understanding of complex issues. Interdisciplinary approaches, which transcend disciplinary boundaries, can foster a more holistic perspective by integrating knowledge from multiple fields. Embracing interdisciplinary collaboration allows for a more nuanced exploration of complex problems and encourages the integration of diverse perspectives and methodologies.

Additionally, understanding the boundaries of disciplinary knowledge prompts critical reflection on the limitations and gaps within a specific field. It encourages researchers and scholars to explore interdisciplinary connections, engage with other disciplines, and seek out diverse sources of knowledge. By transcending disciplinary boundaries, individuals can expand their intellectual horizons and develop a more comprehensive and integrative understanding of the world.

In summary, disciplinary knowledge is bounded by the scope and focus of specific academic disciplines. While valuable, it has inherent limitations and biases. Recognizing these boundaries is crucial for fostering interdisciplinary collaboration, integrating diverse perspectives, and cultivating a more comprehensive understanding of complex issues. By embracing interdisciplinary approaches and critically reflecting on disciplinary limitations, individuals can push the boundaries of knowledge and contribute to a more holistic and interconnected body of understanding.

4.4 The Influence of Paradigms and Disciplinary Silos

Paradigms and disciplinary silos play a crucial role in shaping knowledge and contribute to its limitations. Paradigms are shared frameworks within disciplines that shape how knowledge is generated and understood. While they promote coherence and advancement, they can lead to narrow perspectives and resistance to alternative views. Disciplinary silos hinder interdisciplinary collaboration and limit exposure to diverse approaches and ideas, perpetuating ignorance.

Understanding the theoretical challenges of knowledge, the uncertainties of information, disciplinary boundaries, and the influence of paradigms and disciplinary silos is key to recognizing the limits of knowledge. These limitations contribute to ignorance, even among the most educated individuals. By acknowledging these boundaries, we can foster a more humble and nuanced approach to acquiring knowledge, encouraging interdisciplinary collaboration, and promoting a comprehensive understanding of the world.

Paradigms provide a lens through which scholars view and interpret the world. They establish a shared set of beliefs, concepts, and approaches that define what is considered valid and relevant within a discipline. While paradigms facilitate coherence and progress within a specific field, they can also lead to tunnel vision and resistance to alternative perspectives. Individuals operating within a particular paradigm may need to pay more attention to information that aligns with their established beliefs or theoretical frameworks, resulting in a limited and biased understanding of complex issues and hindering intellectual growth.

Disciplinary silos further exacerbate the problem by isolating knowledge and inhibiting interdisciplinary collaboration. When scholars primarily engage within their disciplinary boundaries, there is a limited exchange of ideas, methodologies, and insights across different fields. This lack of cross-pollination restricts the exploration of diverse perspectives and hampers the development of holistic understanding. It can also impede identifying innovative solutions to complex problems requiring interdisciplinary approaches.

The influence of paradigms and disciplinary silos reinforces the persistence of ignorance among the most educated individuals. The adherence to a specific paradigm and the lack of interdisciplinary collaboration can limit individuals' exposure to alternative viewpoints, innovative methodologies, and diverse ways of thinking. This narrow focus on disciplinary boundaries may prevent individuals from recognizing the limitations of their knowledge and hinder the integration of insights from other disciplines.

It is essential to encourage interdisciplinary dialogue, collaboration, and the integration of multiple perspectives to overcome the influence of paradigms and disciplinary silos. Breaking down disciplinary barriers and fostering a culture of openness and intellectual curiosity can promote a more comprehensive and nuanced understanding of complex issues. By embracing interdisciplinary approaches, individuals can challenge existing paradigms, explore new avenues of inquiry, and foster a more integrative and informed intellectual landscape.

In summary, paradigms and disciplinary silos significantly impact knowledge acquisition and can contribute to the persistence of ignorance among highly educated individuals. Paradigms shape the frameworks of thought within disciplines, but they can also lead to narrow-mindedness and resistance to alternative perspectives. Disciplinary silos further hinder the exchange of ideas and interdisciplinary collaboration. Overcoming these influences requires embracing interdisciplinary dialogue and breaking down disciplinary boundaries to foster a more comprehensive and diverse understanding of the world.

Chapter 5

Factors Contributing to Ignorance Among the Educated

5.1 Emotional and Motivational Biases

Emotions and motivations significantly shape human cognition and decision-making processes. Emotional biases, such as motivated and emotional reasoning, can influence how individuals interpret and evaluate information. These biases can lead to selective attention, biased interpretation, and the rejection of conflicting information. Highly educated individuals are not immune to these biases and can contribute to ignorance by reinforcing preexisting beliefs and limiting consideration of alternative perspectives.

One common emotional bias is confirmation bias, which involves seeking, interpreting, and favoring information that confirms our existing beliefs or desires while disregarding or downplaying contradictory evidence. This bias arises from a natural human inclination to seek validation and maintain a sense of consistency in our beliefs. When emotionally attached to certain ideas or ideologies, individuals selectively process information supporting their preconceived notions, reinforcing their existing beliefs, and blocking dissenting perspectives.

Motivational biases also impact knowledge acquisition and understanding. Motivation refers to the internal drives, goals, and desires that influence our thoughts and behaviors. For instance, individuals may be motivated to defend their self-esteem, protect their social status, or maintain a sense of coherence in their belief systems. These motivations can lead to biases such as self-serving bias, where individuals attribute successes to internal factors and failures to external factors, bolstering their self-image and protecting their ego.

Emotional and motivational biases hinder critical thinking, objectivity, and openness to alternative viewpoints. They can create barriers to knowledge acquisition by limiting individuals' willingness to challenge their beliefs, engage in self-reflection, or consider alternative perspectives. These biases can perpetuate ignorance as individuals become trapped in their emotional and motivational filters, reinforcing their preconceived notions and avoiding intellectual growth.

Recognizing and addressing emotional and motivational biases is crucial in overcoming ignorance. Developing emotional intelligence, self-awareness, and empathy can help individuals navigate their biases and approach knowledge acquisition more objectively. Creating an environment that fosters psychological safety and encourages intellectual humility can also promote open dialogue, constructive criticism, and the exploration of diverse perspectives.

In summary, emotional and motivational biases significantly influence knowledge acquisition and contribute to ignorance among highly educated individuals. Confirmation and self-serving biases are examples of biases driven by emotions and motivations, which can lead to selective information processing and resistance to alternative viewpoints. Overcoming these biases requires cultivating emotional intelligence, self-awareness, and empathy and creating an environment that encourages open dialogue and intellectual humility. By addressing emotional and motivational biases, individuals can strive for a more objective and comprehensive understanding of the world.

5.2 Ingroup Favoritism and Identity Protection

Social psychology research highlight the prevalence of ingroup favoritism, where individuals prioritize and defend their own social, cultural, or ideological groups. Highly educated individuals are not exempt from this bias and may exhibit ingroup favoritism, leading to a limited understanding of alternative perspectives and ignorance about differing viewpoints. This bias can hinder the pursuit of knowledge by preventing critical evaluation of one's own group's positions and impeding the exploration of diverse ideas.

On the other hand, identity protection involves the instinctive need to protect one's self-identity and maintain a positive self-image. When faced with information or ideas that threaten one's identity or contradict deeply held beliefs, individuals may use defensive behaviors to protect their sense of self, manifesting as resistance to considering alternative perspectives, dismissing contradictory evidence, or avoiding conversations that challenge one's beliefs.

These biases operate at conscious and unconscious levels, shaping individuals' perceptions, attitudes, and behaviors. Despite their intellectual accomplishments, highly educated individuals are not immune to these biases. Their deep involvement in certain academic or professional communities can strengthen their identification with specific ingroups and increase their tendency towards ingroup favoritism and identity protection.

Ingroup favoritism and identity protection can perpetuate ignorance by creating intellectual echo chambers and reinforcing existing biases. When individuals surround themselves with like-minded individuals who share their beliefs, they may be less exposed to diverse perspectives and alternative viewpoints, which limits the opportunity for intellectual growth, critical information evaluation, and new knowledge discovery.

Recognizing and mitigating the influence of ingroup favoritism and identity protection is essential in fostering a more inclusive and intellectually robust environment. Encouraging diversity of thought, promoting dialogue across diverse groups, and creating spaces that facilitate respectful disagreement can challenge ingrained biases and expand individuals' understanding of complex issues. By actively seeking different perspectives and engaging in open-minded discussions, highly educated individuals can overcome ingroup biases and promote a more informed and inclusive pursuit of knowledge.

In summary, ingroup favoritism and identity protection are social biases that can hinder the pursuit of knowledge among highly educated individuals. These biases can lead to biased evaluation of information, resistance to alternative perspectives, and the perpetuation of ignorance. Overcoming these biases requires creating an environment that fosters diverse viewpoints, encourages respectful dialogue, and promotes intellectual humility. By doing so, individuals can challenge their biases, broaden their understanding, and actively contribute to advancing knowledge.

5.3 Intellectual Entitlement and Dismissal of Alternative Views

Acquiring knowledge and education can sometimes lead to intellectual entitlement, where individuals believe their expertise surpasses others'. This sense of entitlement can result in dismissing alternative views and devaluing different perspectives. It hampers intellectual discourse and limits exposure to diverse ideas, hindering intellectual growth and understanding.

Intellectual entitlement is a cognitive bias contributing to highly educated individuals' ignorance. It involves a sense of superiority based on intellectual achievements. Often those experiencing intellectual entitlement dismiss alternative views that challenge their beliefs or expertise.

Due to their extensive knowledge and academic accomplishments, highly educated individuals may develop a sense of intellectual entitlement. This entitlement can manifest as an unwillingness to entertain or seriously consider alternative views, dismissing them as inferior or unworthy of consideration. This dismissive attitude can hinder intellectual growth, limit understanding, and perpetuate ignorance.

Dismissing alternative views is detrimental to pursuing knowledge as it stifles critical thinking, hampers intellectual curiosity, and inhibits exploring new ideas. It creates an echo chamber where individuals only engage with like-minded individuals or ideas that align with their preconceived notions. By disregarding alternative perspectives, highly educated individuals may miss valuable insights, innovative approaches, and opportunities for intellectual growth.

Recognizing and challenging intellectual entitlement is crucial for overcoming ignorance and fostering a more open-minded and intellectually humble approach to knowledge. Embracing diverse viewpoints, actively engaging in respectful discourse, and cultivating intellectual curiosity are essential steps toward broadening one's understanding and breaking free from the confines of intellectual entitlement.

5.4 Educational System Shortcomings

Education, while aimed at expanding knowledge and nurturing critical thinking, is free of limitations. Shortcomings in educational systems can contribute to ignorance among highly educated individuals. These deficiencies encompass biases in the curriculum, an overemphasis on memorization instead of deep comprehension, a tendency to prioritize conformity, and a need for more emphasis on developing critical thinking and information evaluation skills. When these issues are overlooked, they perpetuate ignorance and hinder the cultivation of well-rounded and intellectually humble individuals.

It is essential to grasp the influence of emotional and motivational biases, ingroup favoritism, intellectual entitlement, and the shortcomings of the educational system to comprehend the persistence of ignorance among highly educated individuals. By acknowledging these factors, we can explore strategies to mitigate their impact and foster an open-minded and intellectually curious mindset. Promoting self-awareness, empathy, and a commitment to lifelong learning are potential avenues for combating ignorance, even among the most educated individuals.

In essence, while the educational system significantly contributes to knowledge acquisition, it is crucial to recognize and address its limitations to understand and mitigate ignorance among highly educated individuals.

One of the shortcomings of the educational system is its emphasis on rote memorization and standardized testing. This approach prioritizes regurgitating facts and formulas rather than promoting critical thinking, creativity, and problem-solving skills. As a result, individuals may acquire knowledge without fully understanding its application or relevance in real-world scenarios, leading to a superficial understanding of concepts and a limited ability to think critically or engage in meaningful intellectual discourse.

Another area for improvement lies in the narrow focus of the curriculum. The educational system typically follows a disciplinary approach, where subjects are taught in isolation, often overlooking knowledge's interconnectedness and interdisciplinary nature. This compartmentalization can result in fragmented understanding and hinder the ability to see the bigger picture or make connections across different disciplines. It can lead to a siloed approach to knowledge, reinforcing ignorance about subjects outside one's expertise.

Furthermore, the educational system may need to adequately address the development of certain essential skills, such as emotional intelligence, empathy, and cultural competence. These skills are crucial for fostering a well-rounded individual capable of understanding diverse perspectives, collaborating effectively, and engaging in respectful dialogue. Cultivating these skills allows highly educated individuals to navigate the complexities of a diverse and interconnected world, further contributing to ignorance and limited awareness.

Additionally, the educational system may need to sufficiently emphasize the importance of lifelong learning and continuous personal growth beyond formal education. Learning does not end with acquiring a degree or completing a program. The rapidly evolving nature of knowledge and the complexities of modern society require individuals to be adaptable, open to new ideas, and willing to update their understanding. With a culture of lifelong learning, highly educated individuals may become more active in their knowledge and succeed in keeping up with advancements in their respective fields or broader societal changes.

Addressing these shortcomings in the educational system is essential to foster a more holistic and effective approach to knowledge acquisition.

By promoting critical thinking, interdisciplinary learning, the development of essential skills, and a culture of lifelong learning, we can enhance the educational experience and better equip individuals to overcome ignorance and engage in informed and meaningful discourse.

Chapter 6

Mitigating Ignorance and Fostering Intellectual Humility

6.1 Intellectual Humility: A Key Antidote to Ignorance

Intellectual humility is characterized by an awareness of one's limitations, a willingness to consider alternative viewpoints and a recognition of the fallibility of one's own beliefs, holds great potential in mitigating ignorance among highly educated individuals. Individuals can cultivate intellectual humility by embracing a growth mindset, valuing diverse perspectives, and actively seeking opportunities for learning and self-reflection. This virtue enables them to open themselves to new ideas, challenge their assumptions, and engage in more constructive and informed conversations.

Widely recognized as a key antidote to ignorance, intellectual humility is a virtue that acknowledges the boundaries of one's knowledge and expertise. It fosters an open-minded approach to new information and alternative perspectives, fueled by curiosity, humility, and a commitment to continuous learning and personal growth. By embracing intellectual humility, individuals can overcome the limitations of their own beliefs, actively engage with diverse viewpoints, and contribute to a more informed and enlightened society.

By cultivating intellectual humility, individuals can overcome the barriers that hinder the acquisition of knowledge and perpetuate ignorance. Intellectual humility allows individuals to acknowledge the vastness and complexity of the world, understanding that no single person possesses all-encompassing knowledge. It encourages them to engage in genuine intellectual discourse, actively seeking out and considering diverse viewpoints, even those that challenge their beliefs.

Intellectual humility promotes a healthy skepticism that motivates individuals to evaluate information, sources, and arguments critically. It encourages them to self-reflect, recognizing and challenging their biases and cognitive limitations. This mindset fosters a genuine pursuit of knowledge and a commitment to intellectual growth, as individuals recognize that their understanding is a work in progress and that they can continually learn from others.

Moreover, intellectual humility creates an environment conducive to constructive dialogue and collaboration. It encourages respectful engagement with individuals with different perspectives, fostering a sense of intellectual humility among the broader community. This collaborative approach enables the exchange of ideas, the discovery of new insights, and the dismantling of barriers to knowledge.

Ultimately, intellectual humility is a powerful antidote to ignorance by promoting an open-minded and intellectually curious mindset. It encourages individuals to embrace the uncertainties and complexities of knowledge, continuously challenge their beliefs, and actively seek diverse perspectives. By embracing intellectual humility, highly educated individuals can transcend the limitations of their knowledge, foster a deeper understanding of the world, and contribute to the growth of knowledge and the reduction of ignorance in society.

6.2 Promoting Critical Thinking Skills.

Promoting critical thinking skills is crucial in combating ignorance and fostering intellectual growth among highly educated individuals. Critical thinking goes beyond accepting information at face value and emphasizes the ability to analyze, evaluate, and interpret information independently and objectively. By questioning assumptions, identifying biases, and considering diverse perspectives, individuals can develop a more comprehensive understanding of complex issues.

Education systems and institutions are vital in prioritizing developing critical thinking skills. Incorporating critical thinking throughout the curriculum teaches students how to analyze information, evaluate evidence, and construct well-reasoned arguments, which equips them with the tools to navigate and make informed decisions based on reliable evidence rather than personal biases or unsupported beliefs.

Encouraging applying critical thinking skills to real-world problems further enhances individuals' ability to tackle complex issues. By applying critical thinking in practical contexts, individuals can effectively navigate the world's complexities, understand different perspectives, and make informed choices that contribute to intellectual growth and reduce ignorance.

Education systems and institutions can empower highly educated individuals to think independently, challenge assumptions, and engage with information and ideas rigorously and objectively by promoting and prioritizing developing critical thinking skills, which not only combats ignorance but also enhances problem-solving, decision-making, and the pursuit of knowledge across various domains of life.

Several strategies can be employed to promote critical thinking skills. Firstly, fostering a supportive learning environment that encourages active participation, discussion, and debate can stimulate critical thinking. Creating opportunities for students to engage in problem-solving activities, case studies, and real-world applications can help develop their analytical skills and encourage them to think critically.

Additionally, educators can emphasize the importance of evidence-based reasoning and teach students how to evaluate the credibility and reliability of sources. Encouraging students to research, seek out diverse perspectives, and critically evaluate the information they encounter can enhance their ability to discern accurate and reliable information from misinformation or biased sources.

Moreover, incorporating interdisciplinary approaches in education can broaden students' perspectives and encourage them to connect across different fields of knowledge. By integrating diverse disciplines and encouraging interdisciplinary dialogue, students are exposed to different ways of thinking and problem-solving, which can enhance their critical thinking abilities.

Lastly, incorporating critical thinking into the curriculum across all disciplines can reinforce its importance and ensure students develop these skills throughout their educational journey. Providing explicit instruction on critical thinking strategies, such as logical reasoning, argumentation, and evidence evaluation, can equip students with the necessary tools to think critically in various contexts.

By actively promoting and cultivating critical thinking skills, educational institutions, and individuals can empower highly educated individuals to question assumptions, challenge existing beliefs, and make well-informed decisions. Critical thinking not only aids in combating ignorance but also enhances problem-solving, decision-making, and the pursuit of knowledge across various domains of life.

6.3 Encouraging Interdisciplinary Collaboration.

Interdisciplinary collaboration is a powerful means to overcome the limitations of disciplinary knowledge and paradigms, fostering a more comprehensive understanding of complex issues.

By bridging the gaps between different fields of expertise, interdisciplinary collaboration facilitates the exchange of ideas, perspectives, and methodologies. This collaborative approach promotes a holistic view of knowledge and challenges the siloed thinking that can contribute to ignorance among highly educated individuals.

To promote interdisciplinary collaboration, institutions and organizations can establish initiatives encouraging cross-disciplinary interaction and cooperation. These can be interdisciplinary research projects where experts from diverse fields come together to tackle complex problems. Cross-departmental projects can also be initiated, creating opportunities for individuals from different academic departments to collaborate and contribute their unique insights. Additionally, interdisciplinary educational programs can be developed to equip individuals with the skills necessary for effective collaboration across disciplines.

By fostering interdisciplinary collaboration, highly educated individuals can transcend the limitations of their disciplinary knowledge and engage in a more holistic and informed exploration of complex issues. This collaborative approach combats ignorance and promotes innovation, integrating diverse perspectives and developing more robust and effective solutions. Ultimately, encouraging interdisciplinary collaboration is crucial in cultivating a deeper understanding of the world and addressing the complex challenges we face as a society.

Individuals are exposed to various ideas, methodologies, and approaches by breaking disciplinary boundaries and fostering collaboration. This cross-pollination of knowledge and perspectives allows for a more comprehensive understanding of multifaceted issues that cannot be fully grasped within a single disciplinary framework. It encourages individuals to think beyond their expertise and consider alternative viewpoints, leading to a more nuanced and informed approach to problem-solving.

Interdisciplinary collaboration also promotes synthesizing knowledge from different fields, leading to innovative insights and breakthroughs. By combining insights and methodologies from diverse disciplines, individuals can gain fresh perspectives, identify patterns and connections that may have been overlooked, and generate novel solutions to complex problems. This collaborative approach enhances creativity and promotes a more comprehensive world understanding.

Moreover, interdisciplinary collaboration fosters a culture of open-mindedness, respect, and empathy. It encourages individuals to appreciate different disciplines' values and unique contributions to knowledge. Through collaborative dialogue and active listening, participants can learn from each other, challenge their assumptions, and cultivate a deeper appreciation for the complexity of issues.

To encourage interdisciplinary collaboration, educational institutions, research organizations, and policymakers can create platforms and spaces that facilitate interdisciplinary exchange. They can promote interdisciplinary research projects, establish interdisciplinary programs and departments, and provide funding and resources to support collaborative endeavors. Fostering a collaborative mindset through interdisciplinary coursework, seminars, and workshops can help individuals develop the skills necessary for effective collaboration across disciplines.

By embracing interdisciplinary collaboration, highly educated individuals can transcend the limitations of their disciplinary knowledge and engage in a more comprehensive and informed exploration of complex issues. This collaborative approach not only combats ignorance but also encourages the integration of diverse perspectives, promotes innovation, and leads to more robust and effective solutions to our world's challenges

6.4 Promoting Cognitive Flexibility and Open-Mindedness

Promoting cognitive flexibility and open-mindedness is crucial in combating ignorance. Cognitive flexibility involves adapting to new information, while open-mindedness entails considering alternative perspectives and challenging one's beliefs. Individuals can be exposed to diverse perspectives, encouraged to be intellectually curious, and taught the value of dissenting opinions to foster these qualities. Creating an environment that celebrates curiosity, respectful dialogue, and intellectual growth can help individuals develop and maintain cognitive flexibility and open-mindedness.

Educational institutions and individuals can take several steps to promote cognitive flexibility and open-mindedness. First, encouraging exposure to diverse viewpoints and experiences is essential and can be achieved through promoting interdisciplinary studies, multicultural education, and engaging with individuals from different backgrounds and cultures. By expanding their exposure to diverse perspectives, individuals can develop a broader understanding of the world and challenge their preconceived notions.

Second, fostering critical thinking skills is integral to promoting cognitive flexibility and open-mindedness. Educators can design curricula and learning activities emphasizing analytical thinking, problem-solving, and evidence evaluation. By equipping individuals with the tools to assess information critically, they can become more open to considering multiple perspectives and less likely to fall into cognitive biases.

Third, creating a supportive and inclusive learning environment is vital. Encouraging respectful dialogue, active listening, and constructive debate can foster an atmosphere where individuals feel comfortable expressing diverse opinions and engaging with alternative viewpoints. Encouraging intellectual humility and recognizing that knowledge is constantly evolving can also contribute to a mindset of openness and a willingness to revise one's beliefs in light of new evidence.

Lastly, individuals can use self-reflection and self-awareness to identify their biases and assumptions. Actively seeking out differing opinions and challenging one's beliefs can help cultivate cognitive flexibility and open-mindedness. Engaging in discussions and debates with others with contrasting views can provide valuable opportunities for growth and learning.

By promoting cognitive flexibility and open-mindedness, individuals can break free from the confines of their perspectives and embrace a more nuanced and informed understanding of the world. This mindset not only combats ignorance but also encourages collaboration, innovation, and the pursuit of knowledge with intellectual humility. Cognitive flexibility and open-mindedness are essential for personal and intellectual growth and creating a more tolerant, inclusive, and intellectually vibrant society.

6.5 Lifelong Learning and Information Literacy

Ignorance can be mitigated by committing to lifelong learning and information literacy. Encouraging individuals to adopt a mindset of continuous learning helps combat complacency and the assumption of having reached a state of complete knowledge. Promoting information literacy equips individuals with the skills to evaluate sources' credibility, reliability, and bias, empowering them to navigate the vast information landscape and make well-informed decisions. Emphasizing the importance of critical information consumption and the ability to discern fact from fiction can significantly mitigate ignorance.

By emphasizing intellectual humility, promoting critical thinking skills, encouraging interdisciplinary collaboration, fostering cognitive flexibility and open-mindedness, and emphasizing lifelong learning and information literacy, individuals, educational institutions, and society as a whole can work towards mitigating ignorance among the most educated individuals. These strategies provide a foundation for fostering a more informed, intellectually humble, and enlightened society, where knowledge is sought, evaluated, and applied with a deep sense of responsibility and a commitment to truth-seeking.

Chapter 7

Implications and Future Directions

7.1 Understanding the Impact of Ignorance

Introduction:

Chapter 7.1 delves into the profound impact of ignorance and explores its consequences on individuals and society. By understanding the far-reaching effects of ignorance, we can gain insights into the importance of addressing it and fostering a more enlightened and knowledgeable society.

Even among the most educated individuals, ignorance has far-reaching implications for individuals, societies, and global issues. Ignorance can contribute to social and political polarization, hinder effective decision-making, perpetuate systemic inequalities, and impede progress in various domains. Recognizing the impact of ignorance underscores the importance of addressing this issue and highlights the need for further research and interventions.

7.1.1. Impediment to Progress:

Ignorance acts as a significant impediment to progress, stifling intellectual growth, innovation, and societal advancement. When individuals need more knowledge or are uninformed about critical issues, it hinders their ability to make informed decisions, contributes meaningfully to public discourse, and actively participate in shaping a better future.

7.1.2. Perpetuation of Inequality.

Ignorance perpetuates existing social and economic inequalities. It can hinder individuals from recognizing systemic injustices, discriminatory practices, or oppressive structures. Without awareness and understanding, the marginalized and vulnerable populations continue to suffer, while the privileged remain oblivious to their advantages and perpetuate unjust systems.

7.1.3. Reinforcement of Stereotypes and Prejudices.

Ignorance contributes to reinforcing stereotypes and prejudices. When individuals lack exposure to diverse perspectives and cultural experiences, they are more likely to rely on stereotypes and engage in biased thinking, perpetuating discrimination, bias, and harmful social divisions, inhibiting social cohesion and understanding.

7.1.4. Amplification of Misinformation and Manipulation.

Ignorance leaves individuals vulnerable to misinformation and manipulation. In an era of rapid information dissemination, spreading false narratives and misinformation can have detrimental consequences. Without the ability to critically evaluate information and distinguish fact from fiction, individuals may fall victim to propaganda, conspiracy theories, or distorted narratives, leading to misguided beliefs and actions.

7.1.5. Impact on Personal Well-being.

Ignorance can have a significant impact on personal well-being. When individuals lack awareness and understanding of their emotions, mental health, and interpersonal dynamics, navigating relationships and making informed decisions becomes challenging. Ignorance about self-care, emotional intelligence, and overall well-being can contribute to increased stress, poor mental health, and limited personal growth.

Conclusion:

Chapter 7.1 highlights the wide-ranging impact of ignorance on individuals, communities, and society. By recognizing the profound consequences of ignorance, we can develop strategies to address its root causes and promote knowledge acquisition, critical thinking, and empathy. Fostering a society that values education, intellectual curiosity, and a commitment to lifelong learning is essential in mitigating the detrimental effects of ignorance and creating a more enlightened and informed world.

7.2 Bridging the Gap between Education and Awareness

The paradox of educated individuals being ignorant necessitates bridging the gap between education and awareness. Education should extend beyond knowledge acquisition to include critical thinking skills, self-reflection, empathy, and an understanding of the limitations of one's knowledge. Promoting awareness of cognitive biases, the influence of social and cultural factors, and the value of diverse perspectives can help individuals navigate the complexities of knowledge and combat ignorance.

Introduction:

Chapter 7.2 focuses on bridging the gap between education and awareness to combat ignorance. It explores the importance of aligning educational systems and approaches to foster greater awareness, critical thinking, and a well-rounded world understanding. Examining strategies to bridge this gap can empower individuals to become informed and engaged citizens.

7.2.1. Holistic Education:

One key strategy is promoting a holistic approach to education beyond acquiring knowledge and incorporating social and emotional learning, ethical reasoning, and global citizenship into the curriculum. By emphasizing these aspects alongside traditional academic subjects, education can cultivate well-rounded individuals who possess knowledge, empathy, resilience, and a sense of social responsibility.

7.2.2. Critical Thinking and Media Literacy:

Integrating critical thinking and media literacy skills into the education system enables individuals to navigate the vast information landscape effectively. By teaching students how to evaluate sources, identify biases, and analyze information critically, they become more equipped to discern reliable information from misinformation or propaganda. These skills empower individuals to make informed decisions and become active participants in shaping public discourse.

7.2.3. Experiential and Real-World Learning:

Promoting experiential and real-world learning opportunities can bridge the gap between education and awareness. Encouraging students to engage in hands-on experiences, internships, community service, and problem-based learning allows them to apply their knowledge in practical contexts. These experiences foster a deeper understanding of societal issues, encourage empathy, and inspire a sense of agency in positively contributing to their communities.

7.4.4. Multidisciplinary and Interdisciplinary Approaches:

Integrating multidisciplinary and interdisciplinary approaches into education can broaden perspectives and foster a more holistic understanding of complex issues. Education becomes more comprehensive and reflective of the world's interconnectedness by encouraging collaboration between disciplines and exposing students to diverse viewpoints. This approach cultivates critical thinking, creativity, and an appreciation for different ways of knowing and understanding.

7.5.5. Cultivating Awareness of Social and Global Issues:

Education should foster awareness of social and global issues, encouraging individuals to become active and engaged citizens. Students develop a broader perspective on the world's challenges by exploring human rights, environmental sustainability, and social justice. Education can empower individuals to take meaningful action, promote positive change, and contribute to the betterment of society.

Conclusion:

Chapter 7.2 emphasizes the importance of bridging the gap between education and awareness to combat ignorance effectively. By adopting a holistic approach to education, integrating critical thinking and media literacy, promoting experiential learning, and embracing multidisciplinary approaches, education can empower individuals to become informed, engaged, and socially responsible citizens. Through these strategies, we can bridge the gap between education and awareness, fostering a more enlightened society that actively seeks knowledge, embraces diverse perspectives, and works towards a better future for all.

7.3 Interventions and Strategies to Mitigate Ignorance

Efforts to mitigate ignorance should encompass individual, institutional, and societal levels. Educational institutions can revise their curriculum to incorporate interdisciplinary perspectives, critical thinking exercises, and ethical considerations. Promoting intellectual humility, fostering open dialogue, and facilitating diverse interactions can be encouraged within educational settings. Media literacy programs and fact-checking initiatives can help individuals navigate information sources effectively. Additionally, creating platforms for constructive dialogue and encouraging respectful discourse can bridge ideological divides and facilitate knowledge-sharing.

Introduction:

Chapter 7.3 explores various interventions and strategies that can be employed to mitigate ignorance effectively. Recognizing that ignorance can persist even among highly educated individuals, this chapter aims to provide actionable steps and approaches to address this issue. We can promote knowledge, critical thinking, and a more informed and enlightened society by implementing targeted interventions.

7.3.1. Education for All:

Ensuring access to quality education for all individuals is a fundamental intervention to combat ignorance. By eliminating educational barriers, such as socioeconomic disparities and gender inequalities, societies can empower individuals to acquire knowledge, develop critical thinking skills, and challenge their biases and misconceptions. Investing in inclusive and equitable education systems is a foundation for mitigating ignorance on a broader scale.

7.3.2. Continuous Learning and Lifelong Education:

Promoting a culture of continuous learning and lifelong education is essential in combating ignorance. Encouraging individuals to engage in self-directed learning, pursue personal interests, and stay updated on current events helps them expand their knowledge beyond formal education. Offering opportunities for professional development, adult education programs, and accessible online learning platforms allows individuals to broaden their understanding and challenge their assumptions continuously.

7.3.3. Promoting Evidence-Based Thinking:

An effective strategy to combat ignorance is to promote evidence-based thinking and decision-making. Encouraging individuals to seek reliable sources of information, evaluate evidence critically, and base their beliefs and actions on empirical data fosters a more informed and rational society. Implementing educational initiatives that teach individuals to distinguish between evidence and misinformation can equip them with the skills to make informed judgments.

7.3.4. Encouraging Dialogue and Civil Discourse:

Facilitating open dialogue and civil discourse is crucial in mitigating ignorance. Creating safe spaces where individuals can express their perspectives, engage in respectful discussions, and listen to diverse viewpoints promotes understanding, empathy, and exchanging ideas. Encouraging active listening, empathy-building exercises, and constructive debate within educational institutions and communities helps break down barriers and bridge gaps in knowledge.

7.3.5. Addressing Biases and Stereotypes.

Interventions addressing biases and stereotypes play a significant role in mitigating ignorance. Individuals can challenge their preconceived notions and develop a more nuanced understanding of diverse perspectives by raising awareness of unconscious biases and promoting inclusivity. Implementing diversity and inclusion training programs, promoting representation in educational materials, and fostering inclusive environments create spaces where ignorance can be challenged and dismantled.

7.3.6. Engaging with Diverse Communities.

Engaging with diverse communities is an effective intervention to mitigate ignorance and promote cultural understanding. Encouraging individuals to interact with people from different backgrounds, cultures, and experiences helps break down stereotypes, challenge biases, and foster empathy. Cultural exchange programs, community partnerships, and initiatives encouraging cross-cultural interactions allow individuals to expand their worldview and cultivate a more inclusive and knowledgeable society.

Conclusion:

Chapter 7.3 highlights the importance of effectively implementing interventions and strategies to mitigate ignorance. By promoting education for all, continuous learning, evidence-based thinking, dialogue, bias awareness, and engagement with diverse communities, societies can work towards creating a more informed, tolerant, and intellectually vibrant environment. Through these interventions, individuals can overcome ignorance, embrace knowledge, and contribute to the collective pursuit of truth and understanding.

7.4 The Role of Technology and Artificial Intelligence

Technological advancements, particularly in artificial intelligence, have the potential to both exacerbate and mitigate ignorance. While technology can perpetuate echo chambers and confirmation bias, it can facilitate access to diverse information, provide fact-checking tools, and promote informed decision-making. Responsible development and deployment of AI systems, coupled with educational initiatives on digital literacy, can harness the potential of technology in combating ignorance.

Introduction:

Chapter 7.4 explores the role of technology and artificial intelligence (AI) in mitigating ignorance. In an increasingly interconnected and digital world, technology has the potential to revolutionize knowledge acquisition, dissemination, and critical thinking. This chapter delves into how technology and AI can be harnessed to combat ignorance and promote a more informed and enlightened society.

7.4.1. Access to Information:

Technology is crucial in providing access to vast amounts of information. The internet and digital platforms have democratized knowledge, enabling individuals to access diverse perspectives, research studies, and educational resources. By bridging the information gap, technology empowers individuals to explore various topics and develop a broader understanding of complex issues, thereby combating ignorance rooted in limited access to information.

7.4.2. Fact-Checking and Information Verification:

In the era of fake news and misinformation, technology can be a powerful tool for fact-checking and information verification. AI algorithms and data analysis techniques can be employed to analyze the credibility and accuracy of information sources. Fact-checking websites and applications can help individuals discern reliable information from falsehoods, enhancing critical thinking and mitigating the spread of ignorance fueled by misinformation.

7.4.3. Personalized Learning:

Technology facilitates personalized learning experiences tailored to individual needs and preferences. Adaptive learning platforms, intelligent tutoring systems, and educational apps can provide customized learning pathways, allowing individuals to explore topics at their own pace and delve into areas of interest. Technology tailoring educational experiences promotes engagement, motivation, and deeper understanding, thereby mitigating ignorance by addressing individual learning gaps.

7.4.4. Data Analytics and Insights:

Technology and AI enable data analytics and insights that can shed light on patterns, trends, and correlations within vast information. Analyzing data can uncover hidden biases, reveal knowledge gaps, and provide valuable insights into societal issues. These insights can inform evidence-based decision-making, policy formulation, and educational interventions, contributing to mitigating ignorance by grounding discussions and actions in empirical evidence.

7.4.5. Collaboration and Global Connections:

Technology fosters collaboration and global connections, breaking geographical barriers and facilitating cross-cultural exchange. Through online platforms, individuals can engage in virtual discussions, collaborate on research projects, and connect with experts from diverse backgrounds. Such interactions broaden perspectives, challenge assumptions, and promote cultural understanding, thereby combating ignorance by facilitating the exchange of knowledge and experiences.

7.4.6. Ethical Considerations and Digital Literacy:

While technology offers immense potential, it raises ethical considerations and the need for digital literacy. Education on digital literacy equips individuals with the skills to navigate the digital landscape critically, including understanding the ethical implications of technology use, recognizing biases in algorithms, and being mindful of the impact of online echo chambers. By promoting digital literacy, individuals can harness the benefits of technology while mitigating the risks of misinformation and manipulation.

Conclusion:

Chapter 7.4 highlights the transformative role of technology and AI in mitigating ignorance. By providing access to information, enabling fact-checking, personalizing learning experiences, offering data analytics and insights, facilitating collaboration, and promoting digital literacy, technology can empower individuals to combat ignorance and foster a more informed and enlightened society. Embracing the potential of technology while addressing its ethical considerations, societies can leverage these tools to bridge knowledge gaps, promote critical thinking, and create a future where ignorance is minimized and knowledge flourishes.

7.5 Promoting a Culture of Intellectual Humility

Fostering a culture of intellectual humility is essential in addressing ignorance among the most educated individuals. Encouraging humility in intellectual pursuits, celebrating the value of diverse perspectives, and rewarding intellectual growth create an environment where individuals are open to challenging their beliefs, seeking new knowledge, and engaging in constructive dialogue. We can cultivate a collective commitment to continuous learning, critical thinking, and open-mindedness by promoting intellectual humility as a societal norm.

Introduction:

Chapter 7.5 delves into the importance of fostering a culture of intellectual humility to combat ignorance. Intellectual humility is characterized by recognizing one's limitations, a willingness to consider alternative viewpoints, and understanding the fallibility of one's own beliefs. This chapter explores strategies and interventions to promote intellectual humility and create an environment conducive to open-mindedness, respectful dialogue, and lifelong learning.

7.5.1. Education and Curriculum Design:

Promoting intellectual humility begins with education and curriculum design. Educational institutions can incorporate activities and assignments encouraging students to examine their beliefs critically, engage with diverse perspectives, and develop self-awareness regarding their intellectual biases. By incorporating philosophical discussions, ethical debates, and interdisciplinary projects, educators can foster intellectual humility and encourage students to question assumptions and embrace intellectual growth.

7.5.2. Modeling Intellectual Humility.

Educational institutions and influential individuals have a responsibility to model intellectual humility. Teachers, professors, and mentors can exemplify intellectual humility by openly acknowledging their limitations, embracing constructive criticism, and demonstrating a willingness to learn from others. By showcasing intellectual humility, educators inspire students to adopt a similar mindset, promoting an environment that values humility and fosters the pursuit of knowledge.

7.5.3. Encouraging Perspective-Taking:

It is essential to encourage perspective-taking, which can be achieved through activities that require individuals to step into the shoes of others, explore alternative viewpoints, and engage in empathetic understanding to promote intellectual humility. Exposing individuals to diverse perspectives and fostering empathy can cultivate a culture of intellectual humility, allowing for a deeper appreciation of the complexity of issues and a greater understanding of differing viewpoints.

7.5.4. Dialogue and Debate.

Creating spaces for respectful dialogue and debate is crucial in promoting intellectual humility. Institutions can organize structured debates, panel discussions, or community forums where individuals can exchange ideas, challenge assumptions, and engage in constructive discussions. By fostering an environment that encourages open-mindedness, active listening, and the consideration of alternative viewpoints, individuals can develop intellectual humility and expand their understanding of complex issues.

7.5.5. Reflective Practices.

Promoting reflective practices is another effective strategy to cultivate intellectual humility. Journaling, self-reflection exercises, and mindfulness practices can help individuals develop self-awareness, recognize their biases, and examine the underlying motivations behind their beliefs. By fostering a habit of introspection, individuals can become more attuned to their intellectual limitations and develop a mindset of continuous learning and growth.

7.5.6. Lifelong Learning.

Promoting a culture of lifelong learning is fundamental in fostering intellectual humility. Encouraging individuals to engage in ongoing education, pursue intellectual pursuits outside their expertise, and embrace new knowledge and experiences helps combat complacency and the perpetuation of ignorance. By valuing learning as a lifelong endeavor, individuals develop a humble approach to knowledge, recognizing that there is always more to discover and understand.

Conclusion:

Chapter 7.5 highlights the significance of promoting a culture of intellectual humility in combating ignorance. Individuals can embrace intellectual humility as a core value through education, modeling intellectual humility, encouraging perspective-taking, fostering dialogue and debate, promoting reflective practices, and nurturing a commitment to lifelong learning. By fostering intellectual humility, societies can create an environment that values critical thinking, open-mindedness, and the continuous pursuit of knowledge, ultimately reducing ignorance and fostering a more intellectually vibrant and enlightened society.

7.6 Future Research Directions

Further research is needed to deepen our understanding of the paradox of ignorance among the most educated individuals. Exploring the psychological, social, and cultural factors that contribute to ignorance, investigating effective interventions and strategies for mitigating ignorance, and examining the impact of technological advancements on knowledge acquisition and dissemination are promising areas for future research. Additionally, studying the relationship between intellectual humility, critical thinking skills, and the reduction of ignorance can provide valuable insights into fostering a more informed and enlightened society.

In conclusion, addressing the paradox of ignorance among the most educated individuals requires a multi-faceted approach. By recognizing the impact of ignorance, bridging the gap between education and awareness, implementing interventions and strategies, leveraging technology responsibly, promoting a culture of intellectual humility, and conducting further research, we can strive towards a society where knowledge is valued, ignorance is mitigated, and intellectual growth is embraced.

Chapter 7.6 delves into potential future research directions to further our understanding of ignorance and develop effective strategies to mitigate its impact. This section highlights areas that warrant further investigation and suggests potential avenues for future research in ignorance studies.

7.6.1. Cognitive Processes and Biases.

Future research can delve deeper into the cognitive processes and biases contributing to ignorance. Exploring the mechanisms behind motivated reasoning, confirmation bias, and selective attention can provide valuable insights into how individuals process information and make decisions. Researchers can develop interventions and strategies to counteract biases and promote more informed and open-minded thinking by understanding these cognitive processes.

7.6.2. Education and Curriculum Design:

Further research is needed to examine the role of education in combating ignorance. Investigating the effectiveness of different educational approaches, curriculum designs, and teaching methods can shed light on enhancing students' critical thinking, information evaluation skills, and intellectual humility. Additionally, research can explore integrating interdisciplinary approaches and including diverse perspectives within educational frameworks to foster a more comprehensive understanding of complex issues.

7.6.3. Technology and Media Influence.

The impact of technology and media on ignorance merits further exploration. Research can examine the influence of digital platforms, social media algorithms, and information dissemination channels on forming beliefs, spreading misinformation, and polarization of viewpoints. Additionally, investigating the potential of technology and artificial intelligence to enhance information literacy, fact-checking, and critical thinking skills can provide valuable insights into leveraging these tools to combat ignorance effectively.

7.6.4. Social and Cultural Factors:

Future research should also consider the influence of social and cultural factors on ignorance. Examining how societal norms, cultural beliefs, and group dynamics shape individuals' perceptions, attitudes, and willingness to engage with diverse perspectives can provide a deeper understanding of the roots of ignorance. Furthermore, investigating the impact of social networks, peer influence, and social identity on forming and maintaining ignorance can contribute to developing targeted interventions and strategies.

7.6.5. Interventions and Policy:

Research on the effectiveness of interventions and policy measures to mitigate ignorance is a promising area for future inquiry. Investigating the outcomes of educational initiatives, public awareness campaigns, and policy interventions can shed light on the most effective approaches to fostering intellectual humility, critical thinking, and open-mindedness. Additionally, exploring the potential of collaborative efforts between academia, policymakers, and civil society organizations can help design evidence-based interventions that address the systemic factors contributing to ignorance.

Conclusion:

By exploring these future research directions, scholars can deepen their understanding of ignorance and develop effective strategies to mitigate its impact. This research can inform educational practices, policy decisions, and societal efforts to promote intellectual growth, foster a culture of curiosity and humility, and combat ignorance in all its forms.

Chapter 8
Conclusion and Recommendations

8.1 Recapitulation of Findings

This thesis has explored the paradox of ignorance among the most educated individuals, highlighting the complex interplay of factors that contribute to this phenomenon. By examining cognitive biases, emotional and motivational influences, disciplinary limitations, social and cultural dynamics, and the inherent limits of knowledge, we have gained insights into why ignorance persists despite high levels of education and intelligence.

8.2 Implications for Individuals and Society

The existence of ignorance among the most educated individuals has profound implications for individuals and society. It hampers effective decision-making, impedes social progress, contributes to polarization, and perpetuates systemic inequalities. Recognizing and addressing this issue is crucial for fostering a more informed, empathetic, and intellectually humble society.

8.3 Recommendations for Individuals

Individuals can take proactive steps to mitigate ignorance within themselves. Cultivating intellectual humility, embracing a growth mindset, and actively seeking diverse perspectives are essential.

Developing critical thinking skills, engaging in continuous learning, and being open to constructive dialogue can help individuals overcome biases, broaden their understanding, and make more informed decisions.

8.4 Recommendations for Educational Institutions.

Educational institutions play a vital role in combating ignorance. They should revise curricula to prioritize critical thinking skills, interdisciplinary perspectives, and information literacy. Emphasizing the importance of intellectual humility, creating spaces for respectful dialogue, and fostering a culture of curiosity and intellectual growth can help nurture well-rounded individuals more resilient to ignorance.

8.5 Recommendations for Media and Technology Companies

Media and technology companies are responsible for combatting ignorance in the digital age. They can promote media literacy, fact-checking initiatives, and algorithmic transparency to counteract the spread of misinformation and echo chambers. Responsible design of AI algorithms can prioritize diverse perspectives and give users access to a wide range of information, enabling them to make more informed decisions.

8.6 Recommendations for Future Research

To further advance our understanding of the paradox of ignorance, future research should explore the efficacy of interventions aimed at reducing ignorance among highly educated individuals. Investigating the impact of interdisciplinary education, the effectiveness of media literacy programs, and the influence of technological interventions on mitigating ignorance are promising areas for exploration. Additionally, longitudinal studies can help assess the long-term effects of interventions and strategies in combating ignorance.

8.7 Concluding Remarks

The paradox of ignorance among the most educated individuals reveals the complexity of knowledge acquisition, the influence of cognitive and social biases, and the limitations of human understanding. By acknowledging and addressing this paradox, we can foster a society that values intellectual humility, critical thinking, and the continuous pursuit of knowledge. Combating ignorance requires a collective effort from individuals, educational institutions, media and technology companies, and society. Through these concerted efforts, we can work towards a more enlightened and informed future, where ignorance is minimized and knowledge is celebrated.

References:

1. Dunning, D. (2011). The Dunning-Kruger effect: On being ignorant of one's own ignorance. Advances in Experimental Social Psychology, 44, 247-296.

2. Kruger, J., & Dunning, D. (1999). Unskilled and unaware of it: How difficulties in recognizing one's own incompetence lead to inflated self-assessments. Journal of Personality and Social Psychology, 77(6), 1121-1134.

3. Elster, J. (1983). Sour Grapes: Studies in the Subversion of Rationality. Cambridge University Press.

4. Kahan, D. M. (2012). Cultural cognition as a conception of the cultural theory of risk. In Handbook of Risk Theory (pp. 725-759). Springer.

5. Sternberg, R. J., & Sternberg, K. (2012). Cognitive psychology (6th ed.). Cengage Learning.

6. Allport, G. W. (1954). The Nature of Prejudice. Addison-Wesley Publishing Company.

7. West, R. F., & Stanovich, K. E. (2003). Is superseded scientific theory adopted? Theory assessment and belief revision. Psychological Science, 14(6), 400-404.

8. Sunstein, C. R. (2017). #Republic: Divided Democracy in the Age of Social Media. Princeton University Press.

9. Mercier, H., & Sperber, D. (2017). The enigma of reason. Harvard University Press.

10. Tversky, A., & Kahneman, D. (1974). Judgment under uncertainty: Heuristics and biases. Science, 185(4157), 1124-1131.

11. Baron, J. (2008). Thinking and Deciding (4th ed.). Cambridge University Press.

12. Stanovich, K. E., & West, R. F. (2000). Individual differences in reasoning: Implications for the rationality debate? Behavioral and Brain Sciences, 23(5), 645-726.

13. Epley, N., & Gilovich, T. (2016). The mechanics of motivated reasoning. Journal of Economic Perspectives, 30(3), 133-140.

14. Ellemers, N., Spears, R., & Doosje, B. (2002). Self and social identity. Annual Review of Psychology, 53(1), 161-186.

15. Moscovici, S. (1985). Social influence and social change. Academic Press.

16. Fricker, M. (2007). Epistemic injustice: Power and the ethics of knowing. Oxford University Press.

17. Hookway, C. (2010). Trust and ignorance. Social Epistemology, 24(3), 261-276.

18. Zollman, K. J. (2010). The epistemic benefit of transient diversity. Erkenntnis, 72(1), 17-35.

19. Lepore, E., & Smith, P. (2018). Simplicity and complexity in anthropology: Contributions of the history of anthropology to anthropological complexity. Cambridge University Press.

20. Rieke, R. D., & Ballestero, S. M. (2018). Public policy analysis. Routledge.

21. Pennycook, G., & Rand, D. G. (2019). The Implied Truth Effect: Attaching Warnings to a Subset of Fake News Stories Increases Perceived Accuracy of Stories Without Warnings. Management Science, 66(11), 4944-4957.

22. Stanovich, K. E. (2009). What intelligence tests miss: The psychology of rational thought. Yale University Press.

23. Baron, J., & Jurney, J. (2014). Norms and decision making: A moral cognition perspective. In The Wiley Blackwell Handbook of Judgment and Decision Making (pp. 303-322). Wiley.

24. Kunda, Z. (1990). The case for motivated reasoning. Psychological Bulletin, 108(3), 480-498.

25. Facione, P. A. (2015). Critical thinking: What it is and why it counts. California Academic Press.